LET'S WORK IT OUT™

What to Do When Your
Family Has to Cut Costs

Rachel Lynette

PowerKiDS
press.
New York

Published in 2010 by The Rosen Publishing Group, Inc.
29 East 21st Street, New York, NY 10010

First Edition

Editor: Joanne Randolph
Book Design: Julio Gil
Photo Researcher: Jessica Gerweck

Photo Credits: Cover Andersen Ross/Getty Images; p. 4 Bruce Ayers/Getty Images; p. 6 Jose Luis Pelaez/Getty Images; p. 8 Shutterstock.com; p. 10 © www.iStockphoto.com/Gene Chutka; p. 12 © www.iStockphoto.com/Cliff Parnell; pp. 14, 20 © www.iStockphoto.com/Catherine Yeulet; p. 16 © www.iStockphoto.com/digitalskillet; p. 18 © www.iStockphoto.com/Yarinca.

Library of Congress Cataloging-in-Publication Data

Lynette, Rachel.
    Let's work it out : what to do when your family has to cut costs / Rachel Lynette. — 1st ed.
        p. cm. — (Let's work it out)
    Includes index.
    ISBN 978-1-4358-9340-5 (library binding) — ISBN 978-1-4358-9768-7 (pbk.) — ISBN 978-1-4358-9769-4 (6-pack)
    1. Finance, Personal—Juvenile literature. 2. Family—Economic aspects—Juvenile literature. I. Title.
    HG179.L96 2010
    332.024—dc22
                                                          2009023737

Manufactured in the United States of America

CPSIA Compliance Information: Batch #WW10PK: For Further Information contact Rosen Publishing, New York, New York at 1-800-237-9932

Contents

Your mother may talk to you about her plans to cut costs. Do not be afraid to ask questions about what will change.

Money Problems

Lily's family bought a new house. The house payments were much more than what they had been paying in **rent**. Then they bought new furniture. When winter came, it took a lot of money to heat the new house. Soon Lily's parents saw that they were spending more money than they were making. Lily's family would have to cut costs. "Cutting costs" means finding ways to spend less money.

There are many reasons a family might have to cut costs. Sometimes a family spends too much money without realizing it. Sometimes something **unexpected** happens that costs a lot of money. A parent could also be out of work for a while.

Clothing is a need, but costly clothing is not.
Your parents may now check prices more closely
before they buy something.

Getting What You Need

Every day people make choices, or decisions, about how to spend their money. People often spend money on things that they want. It is fun to go to the movies or to go bowling. People enjoy having a lot of channels on TV. It is nice to buy a new toy or game. It is okay to spend money on these things if you have extra money after you pay for the things that you need. You need things like food, clothing, and a place to live.

You may not always have enough money for the things you want. It can be hard not to get what you want, but it is more important that you get what you need.

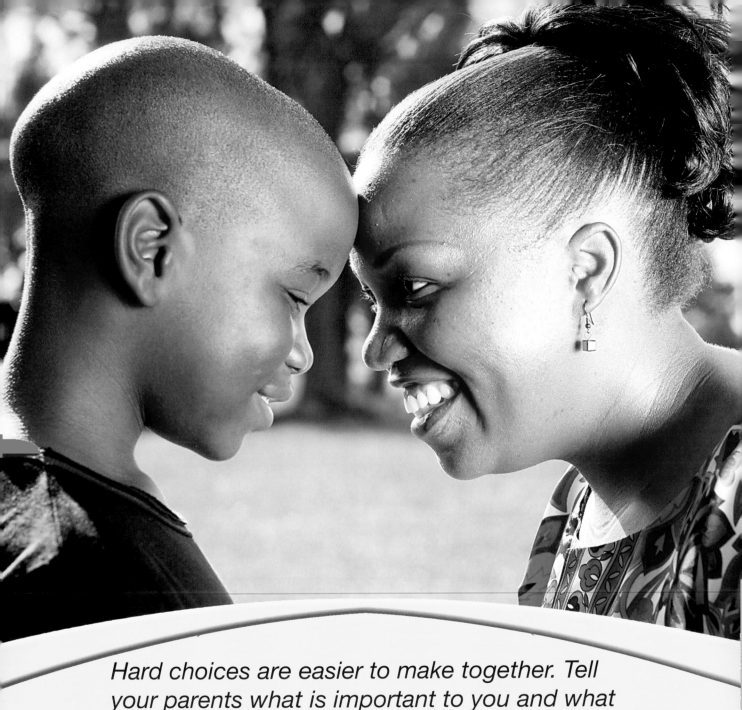

Hard choices are easier to make together. Tell your parents what is important to you and what you can do without.

Deciding Together

If your family is cutting costs, you will have to make some hard choices. It will help if your family can sit down together and talk about what you will do. You may have to make decisions about whether or not you will buy certain things. You may also have to make choices about what you will do for fun.

Ethan's family had to cut costs. After talking about it, they decided to stop eating out so that there would be enough money to buy school supplies. They also decided to save money by going camping instead of going to Disneyland for vacation.

Garage sales can be a great place to find things you need or want at very little cost. Shopping at garage sales can be fun, too!

Thrifty Living

There are many things your family can do to save money. You can use **coupons** at the store. You can buy things that are on sale. You can buy **brands** that are less **expensive**.

Another way to save money is to buy things secondhand at thrift stores and garage sales. Many people buy their clothes at thrift stores. Clothes from thrift stores cost much less than new clothes.

You can also cut costs by using your car less. Gas costs a lot of money. Can you take the bus, ride your bike, or walk? Based on where you live, you may even decide that your family does not need a car.

There are lots of ways to have fun with friends that do not cost money. Talking to your friends can help you feel better, too.

Telling Friends

Ben wanted to go to the movies with his friend Chris. Chris wanted to go, too, but his family was cutting costs. He knew they did not have enough for a movie. Chris told Ben that his family was trying to spend less money. Ben said he understood. Ben asked Chris if he wanted to watch a video at his house instead.

It can be hard to tell your friends that your family is cutting costs. You may feel **embarrassed**. Good friends like Ben will understand. A good friend will not make you feel bad for something that is not your fault.

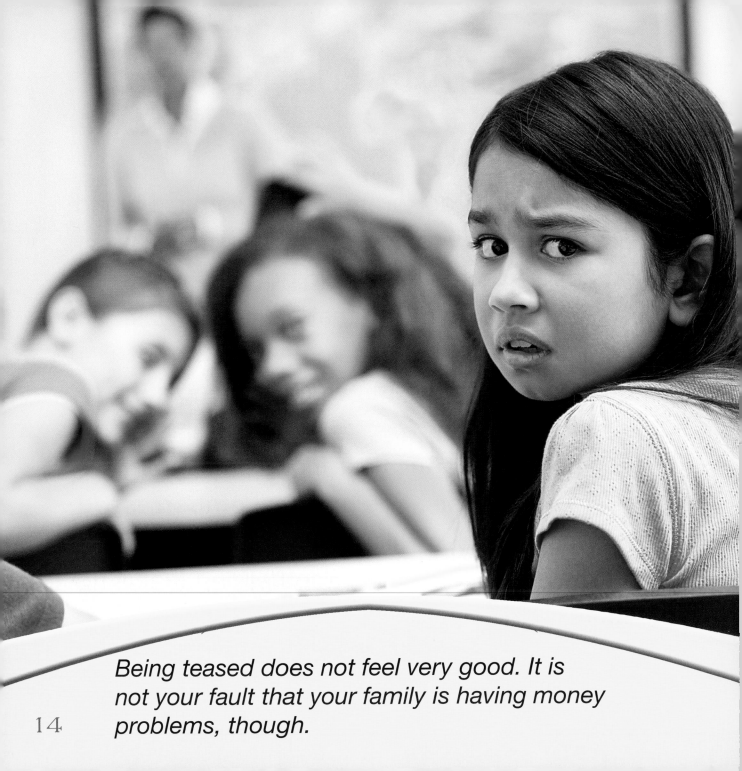

Being teased does not feel very good. It is not your fault that your family is having money problems, though.

Teasing Trouble

Sometimes kids tease people who do not have very much money. Kids who tease other kids are trying to make themselves feel important by making other kids feel bad. If you are being teased, remember that you have nothing to feel bad about. It is not your fault that your family is cutting costs.

What can you do if you are being teased? Try not to **react**. If you ignore the person who is teasing you, he will not get what he wants. Stay close to your friends. It is easier to tease people when they are alone. You may also want to tell a teacher or another adult what is happening.

A hug can be a good reminder that being with people who love you is more important than the things you can buy.

Talk It Over

You may have a lot of different feelings about having to cut costs. You may feel **stressed** or worried. You may feel embarrassed or even angry. It is okay to have these feelings. What can you do to help yourself feel better? Talking to your parents can really help.

Sometimes kids think things are worse than they really are. If your parents know how you feel, they may tell you things that will help you feel better. They may also help you solve problems with friends or at school. Sometimes, just getting a hug from a parent can make you feel better.

You might be surprised that you can make money helping Earth! Most glass bottles and cans can be returned to the store for money.

How to Help

Cutting costs does not have to be hard. There are many things you can do to help! One big way to help is to use less **electricity**. Can you turn off the lights when you leave the room? Can you put on a sweater instead of turning up the heat? What else can you do to save electricity?

People also spend a lot of money on food. You can help by clipping coupons for your parents. At the store, you can help find things that are on sale. At home, make sure you do not waste any of the food you bought. Be sure to eat fruit and vegetables before they go bad.

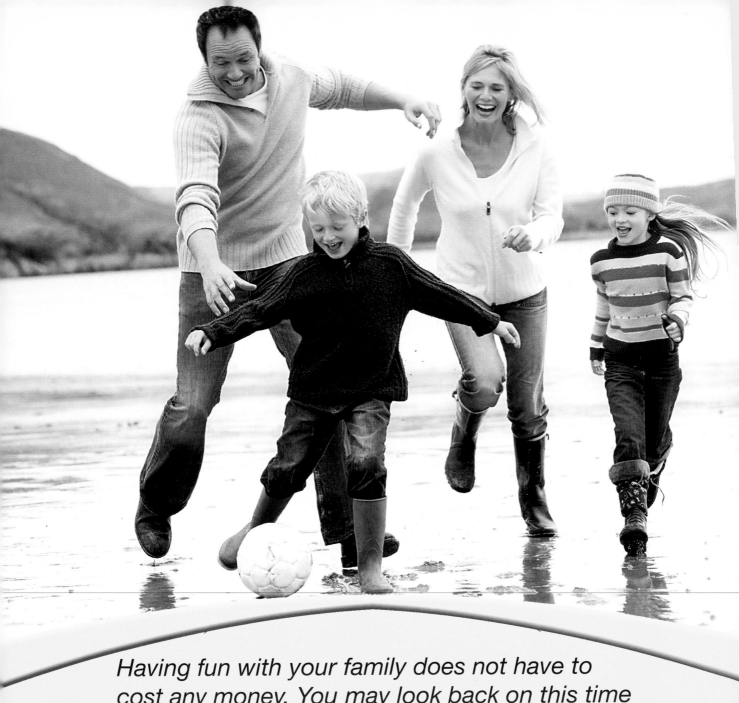

Having fun with your family does not have to cost any money. You may look back on this time in your life as one of the best!

Fun for Free

There are many ways to have fun for free! The public library and bookstore near you may have fun, free activities on the weekends. If your family cannot **afford** to pay for an after-school activity, you could start a club with your friends. A book club is one kind of club that could be fun.

Is it summertime? Your city may offer free concerts for kids. You can also go to the park or beach and bring a picnic instead of getting food at the snack bar. How about planting a vegetable garden or going for a walk? There are lots of fun things to do outdoors that do not cost money!

Make the Most of It

With a little **imagination**, you can find fun solutions to many of your cost-cutting problems. Instead of going out to the movies, how about having a family game night? Cooking together at home instead of eating in a restaurant can be fun, too. What other fun things can you do with your family?

The holidays can be a hard time if your family is cutting costs. You might not have enough money to buy gifts for the people you care about. Instead of buying gifts, you could make them! Many people like handmade gifts more than store-bought ones. Can you think of more fun ways to cut costs?

Glossary

afford (uh-FAWRD) To have enough money to pay for something.

brands (BRANDZ) Products made by certain companies.

coupons (KOO-ponz) Papers that can be used to get something for free or at a lower price.

electricity (ih-lek-TRIH-suh-tee) Power that produces light, heat, or movement.

embarrassed (em-BAR-usd) Feeling shame or uneasiness.

expensive (ik-SPEN-siv) Costing a lot of money.

imagination (ih-ma-jih-NAY-shun) Making up pictures, stories, and ideas in your mind.

react (ree-AKT) To act because something has happened.

rent (RENT) A regular payment made to use someone else's building or land.

stressed (STREST) Worried or feeling bad because of a problem.

unexpected (un-ik-SPEK-ted) Not planned.

Index

Web Sites

Due to the changing nature of Internet links, PowerKids Press has developed an online list of Web sites related to the subject of this book. This site is updated regularly. Please use this link to access the list:
www.powerkidslinks.com/lwio/cost/